WALKING THROUGH MY FATHER'S GARDEN

Walking Through My Father's Garden

———————————

poems

To the Wood-Ridge Memorial Library

11/07

John Chorazy

John Chorazy

Wayne, New Jersey

Acknowledgments:

Some of the poems in this collection were first published
in or recognized by the following magazines, journals, and
contests:

> *Chronogram*
> Fanwood Arts Council
> Inglis House
> *Lips*
> Muse Apprentice Guild
> *Paterson Literary Review*
> *The Slant*

**Winner of the 2006 Chapbook Competition of
The English Department at
The William Paterson University of New Jersey**

Published by
The William Paterson University English Department
Wayne, NJ 07470

ISBN 978-1-4116-8459-1

Contents

Ingressum instruas, progressum dirigas, egressum compleas.

Nesting

I don't know how to tell the story
of a father and his daughter I saw
in a wheelchair, the way he pushed her
that May Day across the sandy paving stones
of Church Street in Montclair.
I couldn't tell their names, but there they were
rolling up from avenue to side street,
her slender body bird-like in a clean chrome nest.
I want to say I watched them pass me
in a hurry, the father tilting back so
the smaller wheels in front were off the ground
and the daughter asking
Daddy, is it hard for you this way?
I don't know how he answered, don't know
how he could, I remember she
was wearing sneakers and he had a beard.
I want to tell you how he pushed her forward
like fathers thrust their offspring off
by hand or absence. I want you to know
about the eggshell's fragile cracks
that grow visible in the sun.

Twelve Miles West

From twelve miles west
the New York skyline is a row of heads
that poke through shades of evening haze.
Points shoot up across the dusk
and like a film I pan in silence
from the neon lights that blink and sway
to the Verrazano's metal frame.
I am nothing set against this weight
and brilliance, I am just a name
at best and barely that.
It is the moment I have practiced for.
The lights glow noiselessly like x-rays
of a million patients waiting for a verdict.
Carefully I trace the cool reminder
echoed by the twilight stretched
between Manhattan and this emptiness -
       you are nothing now, you
       are nothing now, you are
       nothing now.

L

Because I turned that corner
where the old magnolia weeps its branches
down, because I passed

beneath its arms it bowed and crowned me
with ghostly white, because I bowed
in return it shrugged off drops of rain
like glass upon my head that night

I walked the angle of its corner,
where grace and beauty belongs only
to the tree to give me.

Where the Wild Things Are

*"they roared their terrible roars and gnashed their terrible teeth
and rolled their terrible eyes and showed their terrible claws..."*
                                        Maurice Sendak

Mostly, they stare through hardened darkness.
Their mouths and tongues form words unheard,
nothing translated into the language of the living.
Silence hovers over understanding.
No one answers and their faces smolder, unbelieved.

I am turning my eyes toward the faces
glowing quiet in the darkness.
I am addressing every tusk and crack.
I am counting and remembering their names,
each one a germinating flower—a white narcissus
bleeding out an air of death.
Upon my neck, their breath is terrible and sweet.

Bed Dressed in Scarlet

A pine tree reaches toward the window.
Gideon's Bible is open on the table
near a small lamp lighting up a small room.
Faith without works is dead, James writes.
I believe in autumn growing outside the doors,
believe there will be winter. I believe
the fallen leaves will turn to dirt
the way my fallen body one day will.
I believe my limbs sprawled on a bed
dressed in scarlet sheets, believe each muscle
is a lexicon of hunger, know every sinew
is threaded carefully together by sacred blueprint.
I believe the hairs rising from my skin
and mourn the ones I have shaved away.
Faith without works is dead, as the body
without the spirit too is dead.
A deer is breathing in the twilight, its shape
throws shadows just below the window.
I believe in the breathing, each pulse
a transcription of a single symphony.
I touch my own flesh, I am here, I feel my hand,
I see my own form rest across the bed.
I believe in the bone and swell, the curve,
the rise, the ivory against the scarlet,
the paper white narcissus upon a pool of blood.

Sea Changes

Near river's edge the Great Blue Heron
picks away at Fiddler crabs, pretending to be
a man stepping carefully in mud.

A drip of water in a pan of salt.
Miracles in grains of drops of tears.

The sublimation of existence –
clouds above and cloud below, damp fertile earth, cold
air, blood, motion, and ocean, Ocean.

It was the whole world spinning
on God's small finger when water slipped away
from land, mist rising in a cool creep then resting
down before rain fell for the first time.

Hail the shape and size of kiwi fell
upon a hatless man on Broadway who was running.

Symphonic glorious spin cycle.

The brackish tongue breaks
upon a spiny back of land, ebb and flow
                              and energy go curling on
forever and forever, amen.

She takes him and he uses her
reflecting body made of water
for practical and intensive purposes

and when the soft bronze aura of the sun blows
warm through open windows they are dancing
all together and all alone.

Cut away the lawn, mow the great grass down, water
the hungry yard, feed the bright young greens, burn
the broken leaves to sterile ash.

Sing this in the key of D – *change we must as surely time does.*
Tales from topographic oceans. The colors are blue moon,
sea-foam green, and periwinkle starfish. I was sixteen once,
swimming deeply in this dream.

Oh to the stiff height of white caps crashing down!
Oh for the sonic boom of Neptune roaring through a seashell
at my ear!

It's possible and probable; a sea turtle
buoys-up a shipwrecked man about to drown.
The careful toes of sandpipers breaching water
at the shoreline. The sanguine and the blonde of sunset.
Secrets tight in oysters, tucked away in salted sunken treasure.

It doesn't go away until I say it does.

Going Under

Days move quickly past old moments by the lake.
Drunk by ten a.m. you fell into the water off the rocks
where we had cast long fishing lines and down
you went to your neck in less than a blink
and the crash interrupted the silence of the lake
as we watched one another captured wordless
in eternity as you pressed your body up attempting
to walk again above the surface and maybe on it
just like Christ but instead you sunk deeper
in the softness of the earth beneath the water
and then your eyes became serious and afraid
for a moment we both thought you would be lost
in the darkness among the pickerel and the reeds
and lily pads and minnows swimming there
around the murk that had you by the feet until
our hands reached in mid-air like planes refueling
and I pulled you out, pulled you up to solid shore
only to lose you five years later to the lake
of cells that were swimming in your body all along.

O

I took a pen
and put a circle on a page
and it came out clean and round
leaving me no choice
but to try another just below
the one I first laid on the page
that once was empty.
The second, larger, lower one
below the perfect one
did not close –

        what I'm saying
is that second circles
unlike the first and perfect
are the circles
I most often find myself inside,

not completed by my hand or doing,
not round enough by any means
but traveling in orbits
of attrition, wandering unfinished,
expanding, naturally elliptic.

Dear Reader

The young man pumping gasoline
said *thank you*. The sun bled color
close to golden. Call it amber just for now.
All across the sky it is summer.
Someone is praying hard enough to drop down
bombs and already I am weeping like a lamb.
Do not be surprised by this.
I'm trying to make you feel something
close to pathos, a crumble of sage
burned to smudge out devils from a closet.
Green smoke clean enough to eat. But
all thoughts are not a sum of brilliant lights
and that's not what I'm really thinking –

I'm imagining someone
who chewed a breakfast sandwich
and the bread is there between their teeth.
I'm sorry. I'm making a comment
or something like that
on the human condition. Next

I'll say a coffin is a deep blue chair
of one's very own, a perfect fit,
a room with a view of the sea
and you know already what's been said
about the love of money.

Every Good Return

Possibilities of aging
return with reference points
to secret knowledge
of toys and wings of insects
frogs kept alive in buckets
with grass and water
in the backyard
tomatoes eaten from the vine
splashed with salt
seedy wet acidic bites
behind curves of sunlight
bent upon white shingles
of the house

Possibilities of greying
stem from midnights
drunk behind the wheel

Possibilities of turning twenty
turn to thirty and to forty
turn to warm sweaters
turns to soup burning on the stove
turns seasons into newspaper clippings
and obituaries
folded in squares of certain
and specific histories

There is perfection in the light of this
that no one sees

The possibility of darkness becomes blinding

Names and numbers always return
to nothing

Michael

And in the morning
under soft cover of mid-autumn rain
I walked outside again
beneath grey sky alongside
the building at the treatment plant
in Ironbound Newark by the bay
where death took a man
inside a machine some years ago
but the smell is what you remember most
and the one who got away – initials DR
                    who jumped off
the set of 2' diameter screws
that rotate in opposite direction
macerating lime and sludge together
into boxcars bound for Texas landfills,
                    recall the one who made it off
as a machine turned on by human error
pulled the other man down and broke him
and he died in pieces of what he once was
and what his wife with unborn child at home
remembered him as,
                    the other one who danced with death
but this time got away, who dreams
of fractions of an instant in a moment
that makes the difference between breathing
and not taking in blue air
but drowning instead in your own life's blood,
remember the smell and the man down
and the one who made it out –
who walks in a graveyard of ghost bones
and memories of moments of deep dark nights.

2

Let a man be a man.
Let him study, let him work.
Let a man live and die as a man
would want to die if he must die.
Maybe a man can still be a man
where things are clear and a day's pay
equals bread and sweat and a bottle of beer.

That's what fathers said
and fathers' fathers said,
 that's what a man taught another man,
how to live and die and carry on
when back is broken, bank is broken
and the alarm clock calls you up before the sun
and you keep on going.
That's what a man does.

3

And on that day
in a factory filled with tired faces
(where steam exhales from relief valves
 of 18" lines coursing the plant like varicose veins
  and slips into the autumn air with an almost gentle
   hiss like whispers and wings and baby dreams)
a soul is pulled down to its end
suddenly by a machine
turned on by mistake.

One man jumps off, one man dies
   - this is the way it was -
and this is how a man gets captured
and leaves his life inside a dusty building
that does not remember names.

4

On this night, 10pm,
lights dimmed, clocks ticking
crickets clicking deep in evening slumber
(and from a distance come the gravity
of families and wives and bills of taxes
and daughters' braces and wisdom teeth pulled
from the mouths of sons),
lives believing themselves into happiness,
licking their own wounds,
old men reading lines of runes and fables
that tell the reasons children fear to fall asleep in darkness

And how a man sometimes drinks himself drunk
and a man doesn't always know the answers
and a man sometimes sexes strange men and women
and a man doesn't always know why
and a man doesn't always come home

and he doesn't give reasons
and doesn't have solutions
and he isn't John Wayne
and isn't James Dean

And sometimes a man lives in confusion

and a man doesn't always need a woman
and sometimes a man will die for a woman
and the thing about him that makes him a man
is not between his legs
and not his hair and not his arms
and not his face
but it is his soul, and it is in his eyes.

And sometimes a man
takes his cross upon bent shoulders
and will not look back.

And sometimes a man should simply
breathe the scent of jasmine all night long.

Town and Country

Where I begin again
at the foot of another town
another map, one more highway
the latest winding road

the journey begins itself
and the resurrection
sends me forward
against the wind
this is how the circle remains
unbroken, the beginning
of another end

the sky opens
to bells ringing
angels singing on clouds
whisper of blue air

the ocean
and the river, the lake
the fox, the deer
the hen and wolf

the casting out of souls

the sun
holds me close, I am
a child leaning into light
hiding inside shadows

Get Thee To A Nunnery

and so I got me to a nunnery
back to the Christian women's mother-lode
memories of long and sad brown habits
still wondering what rests beneath their robes

growing backwards to twelve years old
when Sister Mary Beth divined
you'll be kicking cans down streets someday
spelling out the haunting of my youth

chastised with crisp wood rulers over knuckles
their veiny hands slapping my head down
with holy venom on the ink-stained desk
pinching the soft red hairs upon my neck
till boyish tears fell openly like rain

and Sister Christine's long legs
dark stockings under a knee length skirt
math lessons taught with one foot leaned up
upon the wastepaper basket and heel that coyly
teetered in and out of leather shoe confinement
Catholic boys exhuming birds and bees from angels

so I got me to a nunnery
just in time to taste the blackboard's chalk
inside the desert of my throat
alphabets of disappointments
my love for Christ nearly stripped by lies and fear
waking today to a soft grey morning of fruit and tea
and crows that speak outside these rainy windows
praying for the salvation of our souls

I Am Not Sleeping

In this dream we are
as bare as goldfish circling
around each other in a bowl
with oranges and yellows trailing behind
tailfins. Our eyes are large like lanterns.
We spin in air instead of water.
Parents hurry by entwined
in silence, without smiles or sweat
they drift into passive disappearance.
No lights necessary, just
our eyes as big as lanterns.
In this dream you float away
as I reach out arms that weigh a hundred
pounds of lead and we dance apart
like cosmonauts lost in space,
our voices caught between
another breath and words
that drop harder than rocks that fall
from rooftops. Stars descend
like eggs from nests and when
you bend to touch the broken yolks
and pieces of the speckled shells
I remember
I am not sleeping.

Morning

I've been thinking this whole thing through –
the world in sweet peril, winter nearing
with its nights longer than days
and the crackpot music crows make
all together noisy up in pine trees.
Such a great, round dance. I'm watching
the cat I've given a humorous name to
follow the squirrels at work outside
the open window and I know
he wants to tell me about his hunger,
how he needs so desperately to touch
the first one he can get his quiet hands on.
I understand. When I call
he'll turn his small head over to see me,
he'll know I know and neither of us
will say another word for hours.

Ode

Here is my poem, dressed
in long black ribbons and silver rings,
clothed in the cobalt steel blue glow
of warm machine gun barrels.
It has the deep grey beard of Whitman
stretched down to feet gnarled ugly
and as real as mangrove roots, its long hair
coiffed and neatly perfumed, it is seated
on a park bench tossing bread crumbs.
At night it peers with glasses on
at stars, singing in the secret speech
of peeper frogs that call and counter from
their place behind the wood line.
It is afraid of people. My poem
loves people. It has breakfast
in big dining rooms and eats its lunch
over Jack Kerouac's lonely grave.
It walks in combat boots worn down
to bone like the final soldier.
The son I have not had holds it in his hand.
It is ready to suffer, die and rise convinced
there will be no more dying. One day
my poem will wake up perfect
and as simple as a breath.

Pater Noster

And the father, what does he do, the father?   --Prévert

I've been thinking long about
our fathers when driving in my car. And
while driving I recall being small and simple
in a moving metal nutshell,

my youth passing by like varied signposts
and every corner reminding me of fathers
driving all along their ways. Different
as birds are different, and every one the same.

Driving in their cars our fathers kept us quiet
in the cold back seats of Fords, sometimes
had us press a squirming foot down
against the slippery rubber pedals

or steer the great wheel of the iron ship,
our fists tightened beneath their heavy hands
that paused to retune a.m. radio dials.
I've been thinking how our fathers

tried to keep things under wraps, slipped
through endless factory dreams
they couldn't shake themselves awake from,
snapped us back to silence

with a shout or back of hand while driving
and maybe thought the way their fathers
thought of never going home
when wandering down any given road.

Parochial

Sister Christine Marie had the greatest breasts
any seventh grader had ever seen.
She'd slide across a room all smiles and vespers
while Jimmy Russo crafted tight white
spitballs bound for front row heads.
The morning David Popek reached his arms out,
pretending to fall, and laid hands upon
her chest was like a dream. No one
would have dared but him, the kid
that took the part of Judas or the Devil
in every catechism drama. And she
came back at him with just one word… *David.*
Not a wooden stick in sight, not one hair
out of place. Never was there a nun like that.
But they said sister Mary Barbara liked
young boys. She wore dark blue slacks
to sophomore Geometry class and smoked
outside. She wasn't pretty. Everybody
thought they knew why her office door
was closed. Someone said they saw her
with a student in the woods. She didn't
always wear a bra. None of us went near her.

Bedroom

My tired head down floating deep beneath warm blankets, my
eyes and ears tucked under... I remember static sparks that
flashed like tiny stars whenever my hands moved quick across
the soft material. I'd always rest right up against the coolness
of the wall, the bed pressed in the corner, hidden transistor
radio bleeding a.m. echo in one ear. Sometimes before falling
asleep I'd scribble on the pale blue paint, make figures come
alive and scratch ideas and secret phrases in, stuck between
the chill of being caught and thrill of thinking maybe when I
was gone someday they'd find and study them like brilliant,
ancient cave paintings. It was never math and never numbers,
it was words added into a new equation that balanced all the
books around the room – Louis Pasteur and Papillon and
Twain and Edgar Allen Poe, The Holy Gospel according to
Matthew, Mark, Luke, and John. The 1970's ready to be
carved in stone, three peach trees in the yard, my father's
garden, Japanese mimosa dripping on our roof and over my
head exactly like a bright pink dream.

Peach Tree

By the time my father took it down
the tree was larger than the house.
Fat as baseballs then, the fruits
were sweet and furry globes we'd eat
right off the branch with dozens left
to fall down swollen to the earth.
That's how I learned decomposing –
   the fleshy peaches that dropped
and turned black-brown in autumn,
the empty arms of wood that hung out
naked to the sky. The night
the dog would not come in,
sick for weeks and shitting on the rugs
and how it put its body down under
the tree and rested there
a final time, somehow knowing.
The morning my father woke me up,
explaining endings- it was best
to see it go this way, to find the old dog
dead at last, stiff beneath the tree.
The way my father let me say goodbye,
and how he finally cut the peach tree down.

Voir Dire

*Do you swear or affirm that you will try the matter in dispute
and give a true verdict according to the evidence?*

        --Oath of Jurors

Behind a distant shred of haze-
morning. Low clouds stretched long
by airplanes touching down, early
steam and smoke goes up
from tapered red brick stacks
and disappears, rolls
apart and rises, disappears.
Trains and people move inside the cold.
Some there read science, and the news. There
they are with books- of what, poems?
They swallow coffee, chew
in sublime rhythms. Voices bounce
across small telephones in mouthfuls of sound.
The Moon! still out, a silver line
that gleams palladium, curving
scale-shine. Silent.
What Ramadan is this?
What Chanakuh, what G-d? What
bright bare star do cities follow? Which Lord?
A man, a dream awake
because of movement. Cars and tires
speed past trees, a film of breath
breathes fog inside the windshield.
A city yawning, and a soul.

An interrupted sleep.
Roads and tired highways thick
with boxtrucks filled with bread.
Whole towns pulled up from rest
aware of something forming in the air.
Outlines of words gather in the throat
and on the lips – images develop.
The lips press and blow them out.
      A beginning, and a return

to what? where
flowers grow wild in golden clusters,
backyards of evergreen and peaches?
The start of something.
Each new startled exhalation equal
to a grain of sand, stars
and cells of Human, irreducible, specific.
The inside turning out.
All curves roll undistinguished
into One, water falling over bones
and into rivers to the sea.
Songs whispered at the cradle saved
to pour into the flood.
I know this. I know what I know.
Everything, quick as the flash of pink
of my hand, a cup for wind.
The clack of a silver key that penetrates
the dark and deepest recess
of the lock, the tumbler folded open.
Knowledge built from nothing else but air
and warm desire. To think,
alone, nothing to pronounce.

No words, not enough
to spill a seed over the palate of the tongue.
Unable to speak, incapable of beauty,
no roses growing, nothing from the mouth.
Unspoken since my father died, his death
being the well my words drowned in.
No sky-blue eyes of his
and anyway, what would it be?
Gasps of language empty as broken shells?
Gurgles of a throat that rasps with dying?
Nothing to put the mouth around, done
and done, amen
amen with a glance of the eye
sideways, down, and quickly up to heaven-
      the turning and the return

to an early fire glowing
through a window, light sent into the cold.
Unnamed colors, shades of some new intention.
Silhouettes stand behind the glass
as shadows stand – supple, body
against body twined in arabesque, a perfect dance.
And behind the rows of houses, light
already sparkling in the yards, framed
for moments between the fences and the gates.
Sunrise! Sunshine
splashing, illumination flashes over
vehicles and chimneys facing east.
Movement, the dawn of something- The Great Mysterious!
Conscious inside the mind.

Hoarfrost on the lawns
and plastic figures frozen to the grass.
Everybody going already on the way.
A soul, a dream. The click of speech
on teeth. The shell cracked open
lets things out… poeisis,
the tick of music squeezed through mud.
He that has an ear, let him hear this.
Let the mouth be open from within.
The plaintiff and the jury, the judge
with beard and the charge of law, the defense,
each one a statehood of opinion
to swear upon the Truth of this –
         ALL IS IN ORDER… AS IS NATURAL TO IT…
The sublimation of the common end.
The verdict rendered by the evidence
         of this Moment –
Hallelujah now and always
and everything that led to it, ineffable.
Perpetual, guided light that pours into the flood.
Erunt prava in directa…Perenne Lumen in Templo Aeterni.
The inside turning out.

Building Down the Wall

for Lorrie

It begins like this - a slow touch
of hands across the table glowing white

with tea candles lit like many waxy stars.
This way, the foundation is laid

and the rest comes dripping down
around it. Next,

a kiss upon the cheek. Soft
as a whisper, the thin wet press

of mouth against warm skin. Form
lips into shapes of words

that have no sound but pulse electric
with subtle animal sense. Push

glances in and deeper down, break
the bread of shared breath, breathe

in structures of incense wisp
that support the ladder of emotion.

Drops of wine and water on the tongue.
You will learn to script your names

upon the flexible arc of each other's frame
and knock ten-penny nails in, pull out

dead thorns, paint coats of white and blue
and splash new flesh tones rich with perfume

of mimosa blossoms onto secret places.
Weld the beams up and then the legs and arms.

Burn the old house down
and bless each other's forehead boldly

with the gentle weight of ash.

Nuptial

And if I woke up startled
At my figure spread upon the marriage bed,
Three cats near my feet and a clock at my head,
Familiar breath at rest beside my ear and day
Already throbbing outside open windows;
If the morning spun itself into a throng
Of yellow flowers and if the flowers lined
The streets in rows of color, regiments of stems
And petals, if by virtue of my seeing them
The flowers pulled their bodies up and waltzed
Under the warm, first light like newlyweds;
If the flowers were illumined by the fire
Of the moment, if I woke up startled,
If everywhere were glowing, yellow flowers.

Rejoicing

I make a promise not to talk
about his illness. Instead
I'll walk inside the house
like a dog walks over familiar ground,
walking, circling the daybed
where my father rests alone.
I'll step up to the room I slept in,
I'll go down to the kitchen of soup
and lamb and through the dark garage
and into the yard and when
I'm in the garden I'll clip branches
of sage and dill and thyme
and tie them in tight bundles
before the frost.
I'll walk back in with earth
beneath my nails, wanting to press
my chin and face to his chin and face
in the embrace sons make with fathers.
I'll make a poem for the young man
and the old man out of silence.
I'll grind my teeth and wring my hands
and shape it out of bone.
I'll say nothing there and wait for snow.

Taurus

What the stars won't say about themselves
I will say. I think inside they must be filled
with nothing else but light, so much that
they cannot recognize the press of night
around them. Looking up again I realize
how quick they are to swallow everything.

After the hospital, after shaving my father's face
and kissing his hand goodnight,
tons of stars threw their white selves down
on me like falling pearls of ice. Everything,
they seemed to say, everything turns
someday back to dust.
I watched the constellations shine
and let the leaving of that beard
swell inside me with wild sadness.
What the sky was like between
the shards of light had grown beyond describing.
How the air felt in my mouth
and on my tongue could not be named.

My Father's Garden

I learned all the things I know
about a garden from my father.
He would turn the soil in early spring
before the weeds came up, folded over
dirt and mulch into dark, moist piles
and sifted stones, carefully removing
that which had no place among the living.
Between the mounds of earth pulled into rows
he laid cut grass for walking paths
and at the end of May he plugged the ground
with plants and sent down seeds to die
their quiet deaths before the rain and warmth
called each one out, skinny infants groping
blindly toward summer light.

This morning I am walking through
my father's garden- it is overrun by weeds
metastasized like plagues upon the fallow plot,
purslane spreading, yellow foxtail pointing up
rebellious heads in answer to neglect.
Sprays of witchgrass bend and gesture
silently, thin shadows thrown upon the dirt,
a sickly dance of slender ghosts motioning
to things beyond my view. I remember
my father's hands, loam under his nails,
slipping out unwanted growth that hid among
the pepper and tomato plants, never troubled
but simply lifting, always pulling something,
his form forever hunched over the plant beds
yet never burdened by the garden's daily labor,
the endless work that separates the thorn
and thistle from the fruitful vine.

Smoke

Because I had a mind full of fire
and thought I knew something about God
I went with all my books and pencils
burning in every pocket
to sit alone at Arthur's, where the steak
comes thick and cheap and large.
That's the time I grew lucid and drank
red wine and wiped my mouth with poems
all night by bar-light and din.
I ate pickled green tomatoes and laid
cherry peppers on my tongue and swallowed.
That's the time I told no one of, the night
it rained and got dark early.
I went to leave a thing there
and came back holding smoke.

Cosmopolitan

Yes I'll sit down with myself for hours
and swallow kvass and count the hairs
and lines upon my chin.
I'll shake my fist and drop my glass,
dance and kick with one eye closed
and shout against the darkness.
I'll go to court and prosecute the world.
I've been listening to Edith Piaf roll
her tongue around the letter *r* again.
I've been reading Pound and Chekhov.
Every day I wake and watch
the orange morning come up slow.
It's cold out there and yesterday it snowed.
I'll wear black socks and a tired overcoat.
I'll feast on words and bread and stones.
I'll get myself right down to the river
and let my white beard grow.

Maundy

I am making the coffee this morning
and listening to Thelonius Monk.
The window in the kitchen is open
and piano chords drop out, jagged
creatures unfamiliar with the crack
of early light. Holy Thursday, my father
already dead and gone two years.
The courtyard, three floors below, sleeps
under the pasty quietness of snow.
Silence, except *Misterioso* skipping off
the fire escape and wandering alone,
a stranger leaving no footprints.

Ars

Old issues of poetry reviews line the birdcage. Dots of
    hardened scat fleck the jaundiced pages, stains upon
    the verses of *The Bourgeois Poet*, otherwise useless.
    Humanity spilled across so many seasons, the eternal
    implication, the undressed recklessness of moments.

It is still polite to bow when bells ring. After some time
    the response becomes habitual- the cast iron invocation
    an elixir watered down by rancor. Clocks and watches
    equally, and just as well. The machinery of corruption
    greased with good intentions. Genuflect and parry.

Shakespeare was concerned with appearances. Consider
    instead the lilies of the field, their tender heads turned
    up like hungry gulls. One a ballerina, its body stretched
    en pointe in relevé, the others dreaming silent rondos
    in corporate worship. A daily exercise of duende.
    Shapiro was simply mistaken- we are forced to pray
    by beauty, not by fear.

Psalm

I like witnessing the pulse of light
that comes and goes dependent on the flow
of widened clouds and the solemn dance of trees.
Watching light on walls appear and reappear
in throbs of brightness through a window-

      the jut and sudden stab that swallows
open spaces, fades for moments before refilling
silent outlines laid across an empty room.
No wind inside, no sound at all.

I like to place myself within a wash of light
that falls through panes of tall clean windows.
Watching shadows pull their shape from hands
and arms and fingers, my entire form
stretched long and gathered like a puzzle
across the coolness of a floor

      but still connected at the foot of me,
the place I press my body to the ground.
No sound inside. No wind at all.